What's Strange About Saturday?

Jane Bingham

OXFORD
UNIVERSITY PRESS

OXFORD
UNIVERSITY PRESS

Great Clarendon Street, Oxford OX2 6DP

Oxford University Press is a department of the University of Oxford.
It furthers the University's objective of excellence in research, scholarship, and education by publishing worldwide in

Oxford New York

Auckland Cape Town Dar es Salaam Hong Kong Karachi
Kuala Lumpur Madrid Melbourne Mexico City Nairobi
New Delhi Shanghai Taipei Toronto

With offices in

Argentina Austria Brazil Chile Czech Republic France Greece
Guatemala Hungary Italy Japan South Korea Poland Portugal
Singapore Switzerland Thailand Turkey Ukraine Vietnam

First published 2005

British Library Cataloguing in Publication Data

Data available

ISBN 978-0-19-919865-8

7 9 10 8

Printed in China by Imago

Paper used in the production of this book is a natural, recyclable product made from wood grown in sustainable forests. The manufacturing process conforms to the environmental regulations of the country of origin.

Acknowledgements

The publisher would like to thank the following for permission to reproduce photographs: p10 Mary Evans Picture Library; p11 Art Archive; p14 Parker Library, Corpus Christi College, Cambridge; p15 Ancient Art & Architecture; p16 Mary Evans Picture Library; p17 Art Archive; p18 Art Archive; pp19, 20 Corbis; p21 Anglo-Saxon Model Village, West Stow; p22 Ancient Art & Architecture; p23 Mary Evans Picture Library

Illustrations by Chris Brown and Stefan Chabluk

Design by Andy Wilson

Contents

Divine days

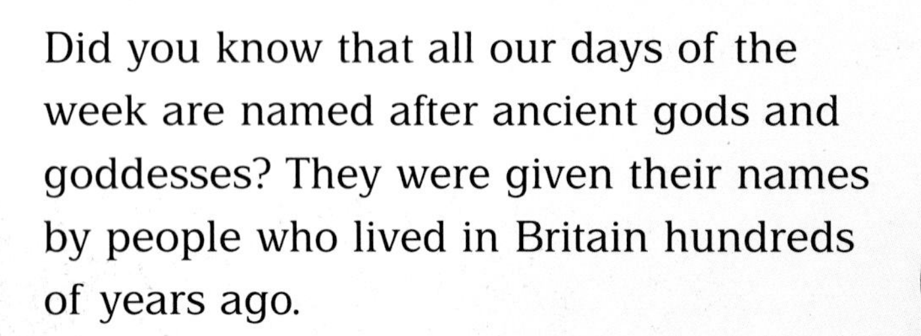

Did you know that all our days of the week are named after ancient gods and goddesses? They were given their names by people who lived in Britain hundreds of years ago.

Six of the days have Anglo-Saxon names – but one is even older than that.

This is the Anglo-Saxon god Thunor. Can you guess which day is named after him?

Ancient Britons and Celts live in Britain

55 BC – The first Romans arrive

AD 383 – The Romans start to leave

AD 400s – The Anglo-Saxons start arriving

Odd day out

The days from Sunday to Friday are named after Anglo-Saxon gods, but Saturday is different. It was given its name by the Romans, who ruled Britain *before* the Anglo-Saxons.

Saturday gets its name from Saturn, the Roman god of farming.

In Roman Britain, *all* the days of the week were named after Roman gods and goddesses, but when the Anglo-Saxons arrived they changed them. All the days had new names – except for Saturday. Nobody knows how it managed to keep its name.

AD 800s

The Vikings launch attacks on Britain

AD 1066

The Normans conquer Britain

Who were the Anglo-Saxons?

Around the year AD 400, tribes of **invaders** began to arrive on the shores of Britain. The two most powerful tribes were the Angles from Denmark, and the Saxons from Germany.

When they first arrived, the invaders fought fiercely for land.

Over the next two hundred years, the tribes settled down to live in Britain. Later, they were given the name 'Anglo-Saxons'.

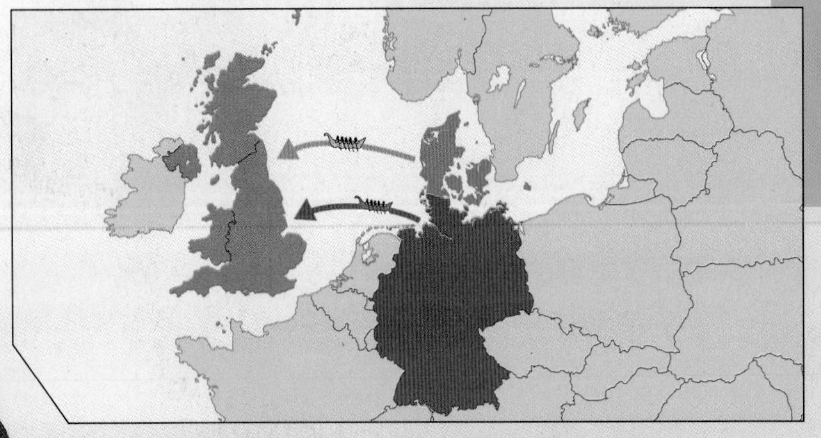

Key:

- Denmark – homeland of the Angles
- Germany – homeland of the Saxons
- Britain – new home of the Angles and Saxons

Map of northern Europe

Anglo-Saxon gods

The Anglo-Saxons believed that their world was ruled by powerful gods and goddesses who lived in the far north. These wild, northern spirits, known as the **Norse gods**, were also worshipped by the **Vikings**.

The chief Anglo-Saxon god was Woden. He is shown here on this buckle.

Ruling family

Woden was married to the beautiful goddess Frigg, and together they had many children. All their children were gods, but their most famous sons were Thunor and Tiw (say 'chew').

Top gods

The most important gods had a day of the week named after them. Can you guess which god and which day of our week match?

Sun day, Moon day

On Sundays and Mondays, people said special prayers to their gods of the sun and moon. These twin spirits were called Sunna and Mona, and together they ruled the sky.

The Anglo-Saxons believed that Sunna rode her golden chariot across the sky each day.

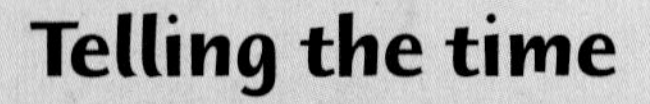

Telling the time

The Anglo-Saxons watched the journeys of Sunna and Mona across the sky and realized they could use them to measure time. People used the shadows cast by the sun to tell the hours of the day, and started a new month when they saw a new moon.

People also believed that Mona drove his silver chariot through the night.

Using the sun

Some Anglo-Saxons made a simple **sundial**, by pushing a stick into a wall and drawing a dial with the hours marked on it.

You may have seen a sundial like this one before. It works in the same way as the early Anglo-Saxon ones.

When the sun shone brightly, the stick cast a shadow on the wall. As the sun travelled through the sky, the shadow moved across the dial.

Using the moon

The Anglo-Saxons used the moon to measure their months. Each month began with a new moon, and lasted until the next new moon.

Anglo-Saxon months were called 'monaths' after the moon god Mona. Some months had very strange names, such as 'Weodmonath' – the month of weeds.

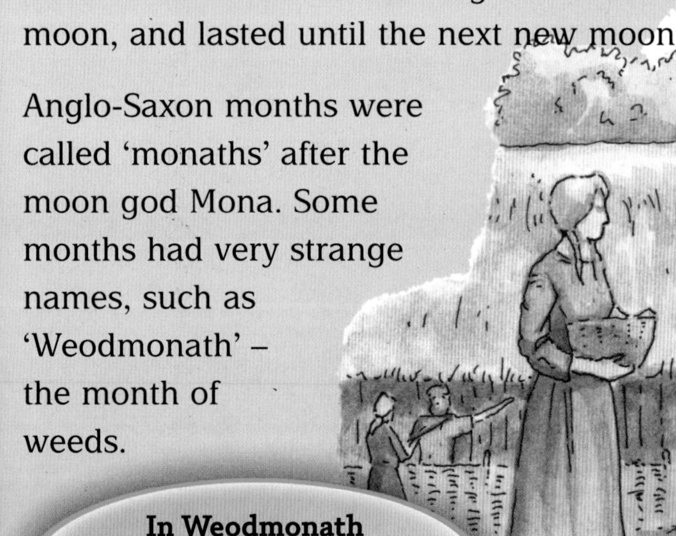

In Weodmonath (August), farmers knew it was time to dig up weeds.

Tiw's day

On Tuesday, the Anglo-Saxons worshipped Tiw – the bravest of all the gods. According to one legend, a savage wolf bit off Tiw's hand, but the fearless god didn't even **flinch**.

Tiw plunged his hand deep inside the wolf's mouth so his fellow gods could catch the beast. After that, Tiw had to fight one-handed, and he still won every battle!

God of war

The Anglo-Saxons chose Tiw to be their god of war. Before they went into war, **warriors** prayed to Tiw to give them courage and skill.

These Anglo-Saxon warriors appear on the Bayeux Tapestry.

Fierce warriors

Anglo-Saxon warriors charged into battle, waving their spears and swords. Some of them wore gleaming helmets which made them look extremely frightening.

This helmet belonged to a great war leader.

Some people think this figure is Tiw.

A magic letter

Some Anglo-Saxon swords had the letter T carved into their blade. Warriors believed that this magic letter gave them special powers straight from Tiw.

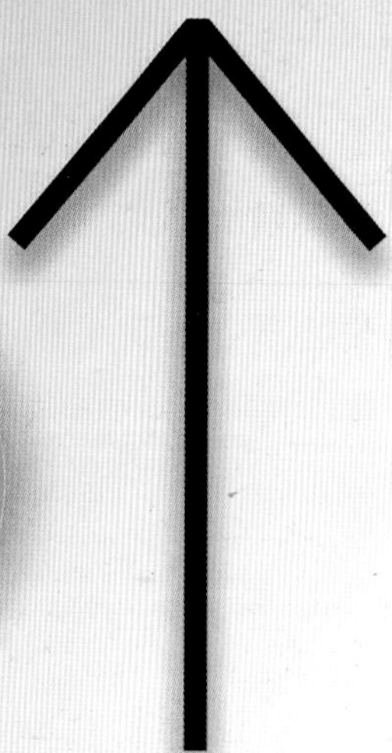

The Anglo-Saxon sign for T looks like an arrow pointing upwards.

Tiw the judge

Tiw was the god of **justice** as well as the god of war. If someone wanted a fair trial, they called on Tiw for help. Some Anglo-Saxon trials were very unfair, so people needed all the help they could get.

Terrible trials

Some unlucky prisoners had to face an **ordeal**. This was a kind of test, to see if they were innocent or guilty of a crime. You can see an example of an ordeal below.

Red-hot test!

Could you face this Anglo-Saxon ordeal?

1. *Carry a red-hot iron bar for three metres.*
2. *Bandage your hand, and then wait for three days.*
3. *Unwrap your hand. If it has started to heal, you are innocent!*

Anglo-Saxon judges had the right to make people take very frightening tests.

Tough punishments

The Anglo-Saxons didn't have prisons, so judges gave harsh punishments instead. If someone was found guilty of a crime, they could be locked in the **stocks** or dragged through the street.

Murderers were hung or burnt to death, and thieves could have a **limb** cut off, or be burnt with a red-hot **branding iron**.

The branding iron left a nasty scar to show that the prisoner had broken the law.

Crime and punishment

Some Anglo-Saxon punishments were specially designed to fit the crime.

Can you match these punishments to their crimes?

Punishment:	*Crime:*
1. *Tongue cut out*	A. *Stealing a loaf of bread*
2. *Hand chopped off*	B. *Selling rotten food*
3. *Locked in the stocks and pelted with food.*	C. *Telling lies.*

(See answers below.)

Sometimes prisoners were left in the stocks for several days.

Answers: 1C; 2A; 3B

Woden's day

In the middle of the week, people worshipped Woden. As well as ruling over all the other gods, he was the god of wisdom and poetry.

Woden was an incredibly powerful god who could race over land and sea.

Woden the king

Woden was the perfect ruler – brave, strong and wise – and the Anglo-Saxon kings chose him as their special god. Some kings even believed they were **descended** from Woden.

Here, Woden is surrounded by the names of the Anglo-Saxon Kings

Anglo-Saxon kings

By the year AD 600, England was divided into seven kingdoms, and each kingdom had its own king.

Northumbria
Mercia
East Anglia
Essex
Kent
Sussex
Wessex

This map shows the seven kingdoms of England. Some English counties have kept the names of the Anglo-Saxon kingdoms. Do you know which ones they are?

This figure may be King Alfred.

All the Anglo-Saxon kings tried to be as brave and wise as Woden. But only one was really great. He was a king of Wessex who later became known as Alfred the Great.

The writing on this jewel says 'Alfred had me made.'

Alfred the Great

Alfred led his people against Viking invaders. He also made good laws and built strong ships and forts. By the time he died in AD 899 he ruled most of southern England.

Woden the feast giver

Woden was famous for his feasts, which he held in a hall called Valhalla. The Anglo-Saxons believed that all great warriors went to Valhalla after they died.

This picture shows Woden outside Valhalla.

Anglo-Saxon feasts

Just like Woden, Anglo-Saxon kings and lords loved holding feasts. They ate vast amounts of very rich food and drank a drink called **mead**, which was made from honey.

Here is a recipe for making mead. Unlike Anglo-Saxon mead, it doesn't contain any alcohol.

Mead

You will need:

1 large bottle of still spring water

4 tablespoons of honey

1 sliced lemon

Half a teaspoon of nutmeg

Juice of half a lemon

Method:

1. *Boil the water, honey, lemon slices and nutmeg in a saucepan.*
2. *Keep scraping off the froth with a wooden spoon.*
3. *When there is no more froth, add the lemon juice.*
4. *Pour the liquid through a strainer into a large jug.*
5. *Wait for the mead to cool and pour it into a feasting cup (or something similar!).*

WARNING
Always ask an adult to help you cook hot things.

Now raise your feasting cup to the Anglo-Saxons!

This feasting cup was used for drinking mead.

Woden the poet

Poets prayed to Woden to help them write beautiful verse. They believed that Woden had drunk a magic **potion** called the mead of poetry, and they wanted to have a sip too.

Poets often played the harp while they recited their poems.

Long poems...

Some Anglo-Saxon poets wrote very long poems. The most famous of these poems is called 'Beowulf' (say 'bayo-wolf'). It tells the adventures of a brave hero who fought two monsters and a dragon.

In this picture Beowulf is fighting Grendel's mother, a ferocious water-monster who lived with her son at the bottom of a lake.

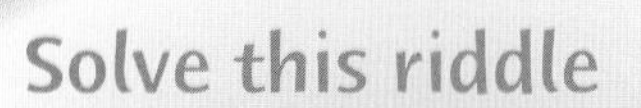

...and short poems

Other poems were extremely short. They described ordinary objects, and worked just like riddles. You can try one out here.

Solve this riddle

I hang between sky and earth.

I grow hot from fires and bubble like a whirlpool.

What am I?

(See answer below.)

Answer: The setting sun.

Thunor's day

Thunor had a magic-throwing hammer that always came back to him.

Thunor gave his name to Thursday. He was a massive, red-headed giant, who was stronger than all the other gods.

Thunor was the god of thunderstorms. The Vikings called him Thor.

Thunor was the farmers' favourite god, because he brought the rain they needed for their crops.

Thunor the protector

The Anglo-Saxons believed that Thunor could keep them safe. They begged him to use his magic hammer to drive away evil spirits. Some people even wore a lucky charm in the shape of Thunor's hammer!

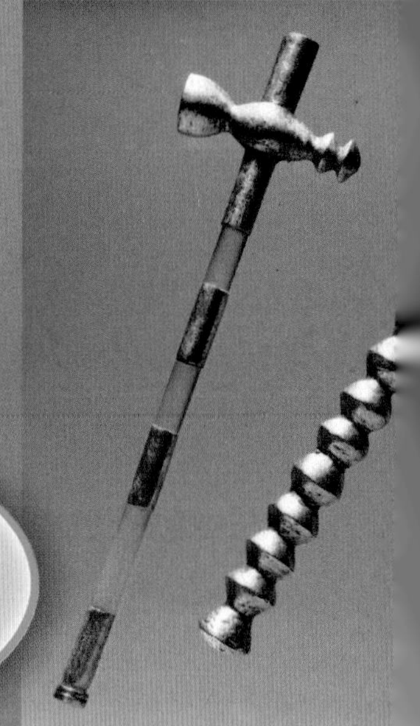
People believed that charms like this would protect them from harm.

Winter festival

At the winter festival of **Yule**, people said prayers to Thunor. They also burnt an oak log for their god.

Yule logs were burnt as a special gift to Thunor.

The Anglo-Saxons believed that if they burnt a Yule log on mid-winter's day, Thunor would protect them all through the year.

Lucky logs

Long after people stopped worshipping Thunor, many families still burnt a Yule log. They also made a special cake and decorated it to look like a log.

Chocolate logs

Have you ever eaten a chocolate Christmas log? If so, you should say thank you to Thunor! For hundreds of years, people have made Yule logs to eat at Christmas time. But most people have forgotten all about Thunor.

People used to believe that eating a Yule log brought them luck!

Frigg's day

Frigg was tricked by Loki, the god of mischief.

On Fridays the Anglo-Saxons prayed to Frigg. She was the goddess of love and marriage, but also the goddess of mothers. People told a very sad story about Frigg's love for her son Balder.

Frigg is often shown looking sad. When her favourite son died she wept golden tears.

Frigg and Balder

Frigg loved Balder so much she made every plant and creature promise never to harm him. But she forgot the mistletoe plant.

The Anglo-Saxons believed that mistletoe brought bad luck.

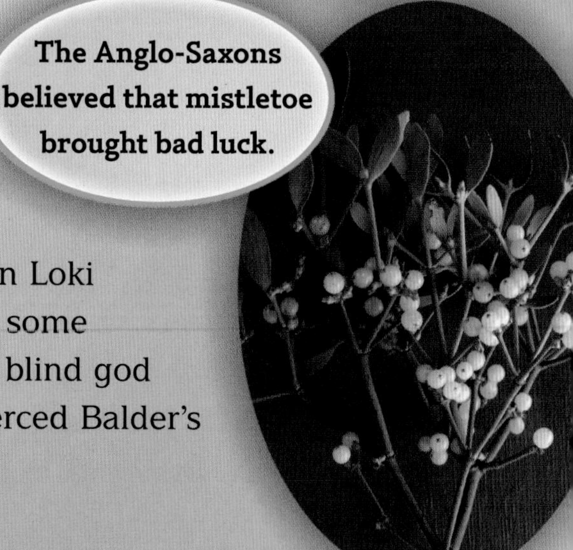

For a while Balder was safe, but then Loki discovered Frigg's mistake. He fixed some mistletoe to a spear and gave it to a blind god to throw at Balder. The mistletoe pierced Balder's heart and he died straightaway.

Care and comfort

Anglo-Saxon women often prayed to Frigg. They asked her to help them care for their families and turned to her for comfort when they were sad.

Anglo-Saxon women

Anglo-Saxon women had to spin their own thread, before they wove it into cloth for clothes.

Life was very hard for most Anglo-Saxon women. If they lived in the country, they had to fetch water from the well, cook the meals, and feed and milk the family cow. They also had to weave the cloth to make their family's clothes.

Life in the towns was not much easier. Some women worked at crafts, such as making pots or shoes, and some were traders, selling food.

Battle axes

Anglo-Saxon women had to be very tough and some wives even went into battle. They stood behind the men while they fought and shouted at their husbands to make them fight harder.

If any man tried to escape from the battle, his wife would kill him on the spot.

What happened to the gods?

For two hundred years the Angles and Saxons worshipped their **pagan** gods. Then things began to change, thanks to a **pope** and a saint.

Gregory's plan

In AD 597 Pope Gregory the Great saw some Angle warriors in Rome. He thought they looked very strong and brave, but he was disappointed to learn that they were **pagans**.

Pope Gregory spotted the Angles while they were being sold as slaves.

Gregory decided that all the Angle people should be taught about the Christian religion. So he sent a monk called Augustine to England.

The Pope's joke

When Gregory first saw the fair-haired Angles in Rome, he made a famous joke.

"They are not Angles but angels!" he said. Then he asked Augustine to try to turn the Angles into angels.

Stained glass window showing St Augustine.

Augustine was later made into a saint.

All change

As soon as Augustine arrived in England, he went straight to Canterbury in Kent. There he met King Ethelbert and persuaded the king to give up his old gods. Augustine was such a brilliant preacher that Ethelbert became a Christian straightaway.

Here, a Christian preacher sets up a cross in England.

Ethelbert made Augustine the first **Archbishop** of Canterbury. Soon, other kings became Christians too and built churches all over England.

Gone... but not forgotten

By the year AD 700 most people had abandoned their old gods. But the Anglo-Saxon gods were not completely forgotten. After all, we still have their names for each day – *except* for one. *That* is 'What's Strange about Saturday'!

Glossary

archbishop – a very important priest, who helps to lead the Christian Church

branding iron – a red-hot iron that is pressed into flesh to leave a lasting mark

descended – if you are descended from someone, you belong to a later generation of their family and they are your ancestors

flinch – to move away quickly from something painful

invaders – people who arrive in another country and try to take it over

justice – fairness and rightness

legend – an old story that has been told many times

limb – an arm or a leg

mead – a drink made from honey

Norse gods – the gods and goddesses of the North who were worshipped by the Anglo-Saxons and the Vikings

ordeal – a very difficult test

pagan – someone who worships many gods

pope – the head of the Christian Church, who lives in Rome

potion – a drink said to have magical powers

stocks – a heavy wooden frame with holes in it, used to hold criminals by their ankles

sundial – a simple instrument that measures time by using a shadow cast by the sun

Vikings – people from Scandinavia who invaded northern Europe between AD 800–1100

warrior – a soldier, or someone who fights

Yule – an ancient festival to celebrate winter, held on and around mid-winter's day (21 December)